THE MAGERMAN EDITION

MY FIRST TANAKH STORIES

ELIYAHU
Finds Hashem

Written by
Shira Greenspan

Illustrated by
Rinat Gilboa

אליהו התשבי

Once there was a messenger
with a **FIERY** disposition.
His name was Eliyahu
and he was on a mission.

A mission to help the people correct a big mistake,
for instead of serving just Hashem
they served gods that were fake.

"What should I do?"
Eliyahu wondered,
"to help the people know?
Aha! I have a great idea!
I'll convince them with a show!"

So Eliyahu
brought **FIRE** from the sky.
It **SHOOK** and
QUAKED the ground.

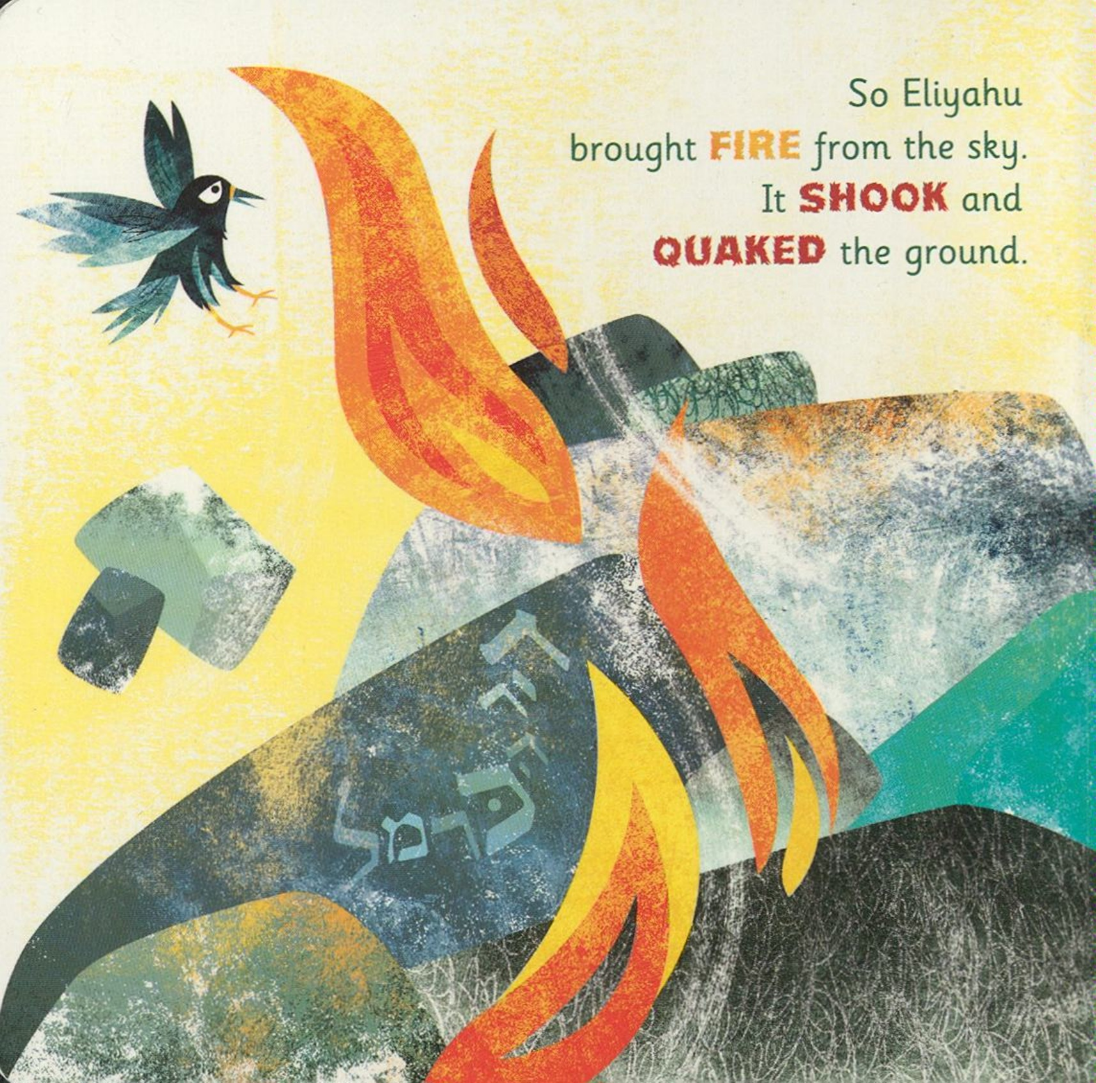

It ***STORMED***
upon the mountain
with the nation
gathered 'round.

The nation gasped in wonder.
Then Eliyahu turned to them,
"It's time to stop all your mistakes
and only serve Hashem."

"We will!" the people **SHOUTED**
as the **BRILLIANT FIRE BLAZED**.

But once the show was over,
they returned to their bad ways.

"I failed! I failed!" Eliyahu wailed
as he ran on trembling feet,
through the sands,
across the lands,
in the driest
desert heat.

On ran Eliyahu, as he wept with every step:
"**SHOCKING** them, **ROCKING** them
did not show them the truth.
FLASHES and **BASHES**
did not help them feel what's real.
Big shows and wonders
did not make them hear and fear."

So what will?

On and on ran Eliyahu, til he came upon a cave,
a cave within a mountain, a mountain called Choreiv.

And in the cave within Choreiv where Eliyahu fled,
a **BOOMING** voice came from Hashem.
It spoke to him and said,

"**Hello there!**" and "**Yoo-hoo!**
Why are you here, Eliyahu?"

Eliyahu cried:
"The nation serves a made-up god.
They turn away from you.
I tried but they won't follow.
Hashem, what should I do?"

"**Eliyahu, you tried,**" Hashem replied,
"**but it didn't go as planned.**
There's something here that you must learn,
something you must understand."

"**Find the answer! Climb the mountain,**"
came Hashem's command.

So up climbed Eliyahu.

He climbed and climbed until

there came a big ferocious **WIND**
and a mighty icy chill.
The great **WIND** wailed and galed
the rocky mountain to and fro.

But Eliyahu couldn't find the answer
when he searched the **WINDY BLOW**.

"I need to find the way," he said,
"to help them all repent."
Then he wrapped up his cloak,
and on he went.

So up climbed Eliyahu. He climbed and climbed until

the earth began to **TREMBLE**.
and the ground would not stay still.
The mountaintop was **RUMBLING**,
and the rocks and sand were **SHAKING**.

But Eliyahu couldn't find the answer
when he searched in all the **QUAKING**.

"I need to find the way," he said,
"to help them all repent."
Then he wrapped up his cloak, and on he went.

So up climbed Eliyahu. He climbed and climbed until he saw a **RAGING FIRE**. The entire sky was filled.
An amazing **BLAZING WONDER**!
A brilliant **FIERY SHOW**!

But Eliyahu couldn't find the answer
when he searched the **FIRE'S GLOW**.

"I need to find the way," he said,
"to help them all repent."
Then he wrapped up his cloak,
and on he went.

So up climbed Eliyahu.

He climbed and climbed until

he reached the top,
the commotion stopped,
and everything was still.

With eyes shut tight, heart open wide,
he listened close and a voice replied.

The stillest voice

the smallest sound

And in that voice

HASHEM WAS FOUND

Then once again, Hashem's voice spoke
as Eliyahu fastened up his cloak:
"Yoo-hoo, Eliyahu.

You searched the WIND and EARTHQUAKE.
You felt the FIRE BURN.
But tell Me, Eliyahu,
in the end what did you learn?

Will SHOCKING them,
ROCKING them, show them the truth?
Will FLASHES and BASHES
help them feel what's real?
Will big shows and wonders
make them hear and fear?"

מה לך פה

Eliyahu sighed and then replied:

"Now, I see that I won't reach them
with a mighty **WINDY BLOW**,
or a **SHAKING, QUAKING EARTHQUAKE,**
or a **BRILLIANT FIRE'S GLOW**.

No, that's not where the way back
to the one Hashem is found.

Only through the closeness
of the stillest, smallest sound
will the nation finally do
a full Teshuvah and repent."

Then he wrapped up his cloak, and on he went.

GUIDE FOR GROWN-UPS

The Koren **My First Tanakh Stories** brings the characters and wisdom of Torah to an early-childhood audience. Engaging with Tanakh stories from a young age with a trusted grown-up sets a child's foundation for future learning and values development. With a story loyal to the Tanakh text and beautiful illustrations, every page is designed to spark an intergenerational discussion of Torah values. Below are some ways this book can be used to foster these conversations.

CONSIDER THE TEXT

Eliyahu looks for Hashem in the wind, earthquake, and fire. Where else are these three things part of the story?

How come the words get smaller as Eliyahu reaches the top of the mountain?

What can YOU do to get someone to listen to what you have to say?

What can someone do to get YOUR attention?

CONSIDER THE ART

What clothing does Eliyahu wear? What do his clothes tell us about him?

In which part of the story are the colors darkest? In which part are they brightest?

Can you find the raven throughout the book? How does she change from page to page?

CONSIDER THE CHARACTER

If you could speak to Eliyahu, what would you say to him?

What emotions does Eliyahu experience during this story?

What lesson does Hashem teach Eliyahu?

Want to learn more?

Check out I Melakhim (Kings) 18 –19, which the telling of this story is based upon.

A **GLOSSARY** of some terms and images in developmentally appropriate language to help guide your discussions:

אֵלִיָּהוּ הַתִּשְׁבִּי **"Eliyahu the Tishbite"**

The first illustration in the book uses these words to introduce Eliyahu because it is also the way that the Tanakh introduces him (I Melakhim 17:1).

Disposition – things about a character that make them who they are.

Hashem – This is a name we often use when talking about God in Hebrew (because we don't want to say the actual name of Hashem, which is very holy). It literally means "the name" in Hebrew.

Serve Hashem – to do everything Hashem asks of us, like following/doing the mitzvot (commandments).

הַר הַכַּרְמֶל **"Mount Carmel"**

This is where Eliyahu tried to help the people learn to only serve Hashem (I Melakhim 18). Even though that was a long time ago, you can visit Mount Carmel today in the Israeli city of Haifa.

Repent – to show feeling sorry for doing something wrong and working hard to do the right thing instead.

קוֹל דְּמָמָה דַקָּה **"A still, small voice."**

(I Melakhim 19:12). Even a small sound can share a big message.

מַה־לְּךָ פֹה אֵלִיָּהוּ **"Why are you here, Eliyahu?"**

These words of Hashem come at the beginning and the end of Eliyahu's experience at Mount Choreiv (I Melakhim 19:9,13).

How can a person know that they've grown? For measuring how tall someone's grown, they may stand in the same spot and mark their height to see how it has changed over time. For measuring how much someone has learned, consider how their response to the same question or greeting has changed over time.

Teshuvah – the Hebrew word for repentance, from the Hebrew word meaning "to return."

Once there was a messenger
with a **FIERY** disposition.
His name was Eliyahu
and he was on a mission.

The Koren *My First Tanakh Stories* brings the stories and wisdom of Tanakh to an early childhood audience.

Rabbi Dr. Daniel Rose, *Director of Education*

Tani Bayer, *Art Director*

Anna Solemeni, *Editor*

Written by Shira Greenspan

Illustrated by Rinat Gilboa

Printed in Turkey.

www.korenpub.com

USD $9.95/UK £10/CAD $12.95

ISBN 978-965-7812-04-4

9 789657 812044 50995>